# The ECG made easy

# The ECG
# made easy

**John R. Hampton** DM, DPhil, FRCP
Professor of Cardiology
University of Nottingham, Nottingham, UK

THIRD EDITION

Churchill Livingstone

EDINBURGH LONDON MELBOURNE AND NEW YORK 1986

CHURCHILL LIVINGSTONE
Medical Division of Longman Group UK Limited

Distributed in the United States of America by Churchill Livingstone
Inc., 1560 Broadway, New York, N.Y. 10036, and by associated
companies, branches and representatives throughout the world.

First edition 1973
Second edition 1980
Third edition 1986
  Reprinted 1987
  Reprinted 1991

ISBN 0-443-03984-4

British Library Cataloguing in Publication Data
Hampton, John R.
   The E.C.G. made easy. — 3rd ed.
   1. Arrhythmia — Diagnosis 2. Electrocardiography
   I. Title
   616.1'2807547        RC685.A65

Library of Congress Cataloging in Publication Data
Hampton, John R.
   The ECG made easy.
   Rev. ed. of: The E.C.G. made easy. 2nd ed. 1980.
   Includes index.
   1. Electrocardiography.   2. Heart — Disease —
Diagnosis.   I. Hampton, John R.   E.C.G. made easy.
II. Title   III. Title: E.C.G. made easy.
[DNLM: 1. Electrocardiography.   WG 140 H232e]
RC683.5.E5H3     1985      616.1'207547      85-7739


Produced by Longman Singapore Publishers (Pte) Ltd
Printed in Singapore

# Preface

In a patient with heart disease the ECG should be
thought of as an extension of the history and physical
examination. It is essential for the accurate diagnosis
of disorders of cardiac rhythm and it is helpful in the
diagnosis of chest pain. The ECG also gives some
information about the amount of work the individual
chambers of the heart have to do. Because the ECG is
such a useful tool it should be understood and used
by general practitioners, medical students, nurses in
coronary care units, and ambulance crews manning
emergency services, and this book is written for them.

Increasing interest in cardiac arrhythmias has
brought greater understanding of the physiology
underlying normal and abnormal electrocardiograms,
and also a greater complexity of books on the subject.
This book makes no pretensions of completeness,
only of simplicity. Most people drive cars without
understanding much of what goes on under the
bonnet, and most people can make use of an
electrocardiogram without getting too involved in its
complexities. In other words, this book is for
gardeners and not for botanists. It is not concerned
with the management of patients with heart disease,

but as a practitioner may wish to carry it tucked into his ECG recorder, the most basic management of arrhythmias has been included in the flow diagram at the end of chapter 3.

It is more than 10 years since this book was first published, and approximately 100 000 copies of the first two editions have been sold. In this third edition the text has been altered a little, aiming as before at simplicity and practical use rather than theory. All the figures are completely new, and for them I gratefully acknowledge the help of Mr G. Lyth.

*Nottingham, 1986*                                                    J.H.

# Contents

*Chapter 1*
# What the ECG is about

## Principles

1   The ECG is easy to understand.
2   Most abnormalities of the ECG are amenable to reason.

### The electricity of the heart

The contraction of any muscle is associated with electrical changes called 'depolarisation', and these changes can be detected by electrodes attached to the surface of the body. Since all muscular contraction will be detected the electrical changes associated with contraction of the heart muscle will only be clear if the patient is fully relaxed and no skeletal muscles are contracting.

Although the heart has four chambers, from the electrical point of view it can be thought of as having only two, for the two atria contract together and then the two ventricles contract together.

The muscle mass of the atria is relatively small and the electrical change accompanying their contraction is therefore small. Contraction of the atria causes the ECG wave called 'P'. Since the ventricular mass is large there is a large deflection of the ECG when the ventricles contract and this is called the 'QRS' complex. The 'T' wave of the ECG is caused by the return of this ventricular mass to the resting electrical state (repolarisation).

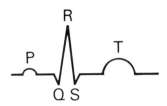

## Definitions

The different parts of the QRS complex are arbitrarily labelled. If the first deflection is downwards, it is called a Q wave.

A deflection upwards is called an R wave,

— whether it is preceded by a Q or not.

Any deflection below the baseline following an R wave is called an S wave,

— whether there has been a preceding Q or not.

## The wiring diagram of the heart

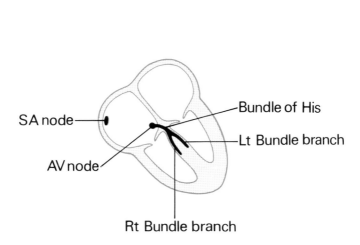

The electrical discharge for each cardiac cycle starts in a special area of the right atrium called the 'sinoatrial' (SA) node. Depolarisation then spreads through the atrial muscle fibres. There is a delay while depolarisation spreads through another special area in the atrium, the atrioventricular node (also called the 'AV node', or sometimes just 'the node'.) Thereafter conduction is very rapid down specialised conduction tissue: first a single pathway, the 'bundle of His' and then this divides in the septum between the ventricles into right and left bundle branches. The left bundle branch itself divides into two. Within the mass of ventricular muscle conduction spreads rapidly through specialised tissue called 'Purkinje fibres'.

## Times and speeds

It is a fundamental principle of ECG machines that they all run at a standard rate and they use paper with standard squares. Each large square is equivalent to 0.2 seconds, so there are 5 large squares per second, and 300 per minute. So an ECG event, such as a QRS complex, occurring once per large square is occurring at a rate of 300 per minute. The heart rate can be calculated rapidly by remembering this sequence: If the R–R interval is:

1 large square, the rate is 300/min
2    "        "      "    "   "  150/min
3    "        "      "    "   "  100/min
4    "        "      "    "   "   75/min
5    "        "      "    "   "   60/min
6    "        "      "    "   "   50/min

1 small square =
0.04 s

1 large sqare =
0.2 s

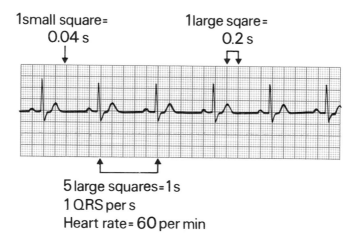

5 large squares = 1 s
1 QRS per s
Heart rate = 60 per min

Just as the length of paper between R waves gives the heart rate, so the distance between the different parts of the P–QRS–T complex shows the time taken for conduction to spread through different parts of the heart.

The PR interval is the time taken for excitation to spread from the SA node, through the atrial muscle and the AV node, down the bundle of His and into the ventricular muscle. Most of the time is taken up by delay in the AV node. The normal PR interval is 0.12–0.2 s (3–5 small squares). If the PR interval is very short, either the atria have been depolarised from close to the AV node, or there is an abnormality of conduction from the atria to the ventricles.

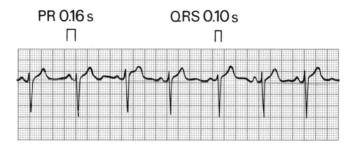

The duration of the QRS complex shows how long excitation takes to spread through the ventricles. The QRS duration is normally 0.12 s (three small squares)

or less but any abnormality of conduction takes longer, and causes widened QRS complexes.

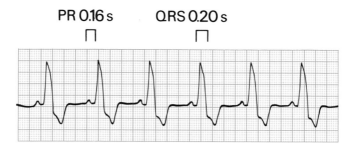

## Recording an ECG

The word 'lead' is used in a rather confusing way in ECG recording. Sometimes it is used to mean the pieces of wire that connect the patient to the ECG recorder. Properly, a 'lead' is an electrical picture of the heart.

The electrical signal is detected at the surface of the body through five electrodes, one attached to each limb and one held by suction to the front of the chest and moved to different positions. Good electrical contact between the electrodes and skin is essential, and this is achieved either by rubbing electrode jelly into the skin or, with some recorders, by using wet pads. It may be necessary to shave the chest.

The ECG recorder compares the electrical events detected in the different electrodes, and these comparisons 'look at' the heart from different directions. Thus when the recorder is set to 'lead 1' it is comparing the electrical events detected by the electrodes attached to the right and left arms. It is not necessary to remember which electrodes are involved in which leads, but it is essential that the electrodes are properly attached, with the wires labelled 'LA' and 'RA' connected to the left and right arms and those labelled 'LL' and 'RL' to the left and right legs. As we shall see, the ECG is made up of characteristic pictures and the record as a whole is almost uninterpretable if the electrodes are wrongly attached.

## Calibration

A limited amount of information is provided by the height of the P, QRS and T waves, provided the machine is properly calibrated. A standard signal of 1 mV should move the stylus vertically 1 cm (2 large squares), and this 'calibration' signal should be included with every record.

### CALIBRATION

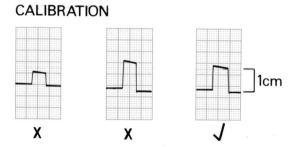

When the machine is properly calibrated, tall P waves indicate right atrial hypertrophy, tall R waves in the left ventricular leads (see Chapter 4) may be due to left ventricular hypertrophy, and tall T waves sometimes indicate hyperkalaemia. Small complexes may indicate a pericardial effusion.

## The 12-lead ECG

ECG interpretation is easy if you remember the directions from which the various leads 'look at' the heart. The six 'standard' leads, which are recorded from the electrodes attached to the limbs, can be thought of as looking at the heart in a vertical plane (that is, from the sides or the feet).

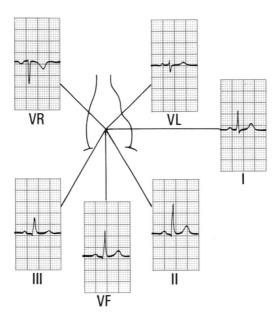

Fig. 1.12

Thus leads I, II and VL look at the left lateral surface of the heart, III and VF at the inferior surface, and VR looks at the right atrium.

The V lead is attached to the chest wall by means of a suction electrode, and recordings are made from six positions overlying the 4th and 5th rib spaces.

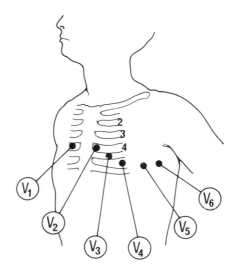

The 6 V leads look at the heart in a horizontal plane from the front and the left side.

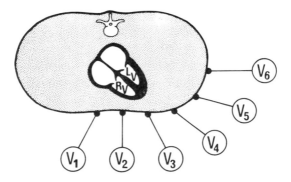

Thus leads $V_1$ and $V_2$ look at the right ventricle, $V_3$ and $V_4$ look at the septum between the ventricles and the anterior wall of the left ventricle, and $V_5$ and $V_6$ look at the anterior and lateral walls of the left ventricle.

*So, when making a recording:*

1   *The patient must lie down and relax (prevent muscle tremor)*
2   *Connect up the limb electrodes, making certain that each is applied to the correct limb*
3   *Calibrate the record with the 1 mV signal*
4   *Record the six standard leads — three or four complexes are sufficient for each*
5   *Record the six V leads*

## The shape of the QRS complex

*1   The QRS in the limb leads*

The ECG machine is arranged so that when a depolarisation wave spreads towards a lead the stylus moves upwards and when it spreads away from the lead the stylus moves downwards.

Depolarisation spreads through the heart in many directions at once, but the deflection of the QRS complex shows the average direction in which the wave of depolarisation is spreading.

If the QRS is predominantly upwards (that is, the R wave is greater than the S wave), the depolarisation is moving towards that lead.

If predominantly downwards (S greater than R), the depolarisation is moving away.

When the depolarisation wave is moving at right angles to the lead, then R and S waves are equal.

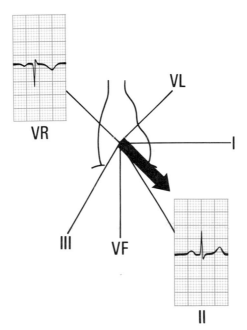

Q waves have a special significance which we shall discuss later.

VR and II look at the heart from opposite directions. Seen from the front, the depolarising wave normally spreads down from 11 o'clock to 5 o'clock so the deflections in VR are normally mainly downwards and in II mainly upwards.

The average direction of spread of the depolarisation wave through the ventricles as seen from the front is called the *cardiac axis*, and it is useful to decide whether this axis is in a normal direction or not. The axis can be derived from the QRS complex in leads, I, II and III.

The normal 11 o'clock–5 o'clock axis means that the depolarising wave is spreading towards leads I, II and III and is therefore associated with a predominantly upward deflection in all these leads; the deflection will be greater in II than I or III.

## NORMAL AXIS

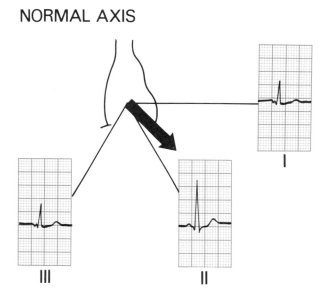

If the right ventricle becomes hypertrophied the axis will swing towards the right: the deflection in I becomes negative and the deflection in III will become most positive. This is called *right axis deviation*, and it is associated mainly with pulmonary conditions that put a strain on the right side of the heart, and with congenital heart disorders.

## RIGHT AXIS DEVIATION

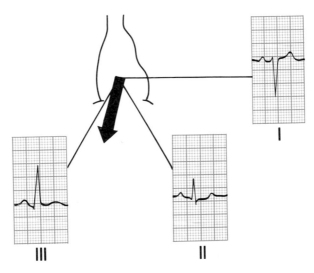

When the left ventricle becomes hypertrophied the axis may swing to the left, so that the QRS becomes predominantly negative in III. *Left axis deviation* is not significant until the QRS deflection is also predominantly negative in II.

## LEFT AXIS DEVIATION

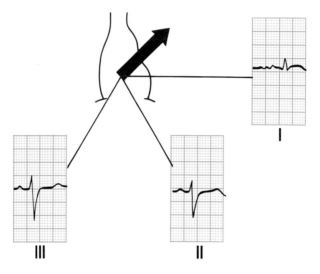

In the case of left axis deviation the problem is usually due to a conduction defect rather than to the increased bulk of left ventricular muscle (see ch 2).

Right and left axis deviation of themselves are seldom significant — minor degrees occur respectively in long, thin and short, fat individuals — but their presence should alert you to look for other signs of right and left ventricular hypertrophy (chapter 4).

## 2   The QRS in the V leads

The shape of the QRS complex in the chest (V) leads is determined by two things.

1   The septum between the ventricles is depolarised first, and the depolarisation wave spreads across the septum from left to right.

2   In the normal heart there is more muscle in the wall of the left ventricle than in the right ventricle, and the left ventricle therefore exerts more influence on the ECG pattern than the right ventricle.

The leads $V_1$ and $V_2$ are 'looking at' the right ventricle. Leads $V_3$ and $V_4$ look at the septum and $V_5$ and $V_6$ at the left ventricle.

In a right ventricular lead the deflection is first upwards (R wave) as the septum is depolarised. In a left ventricular lead the opposite pattern is seen: there is a small downward deflection ('septal' Q wave).

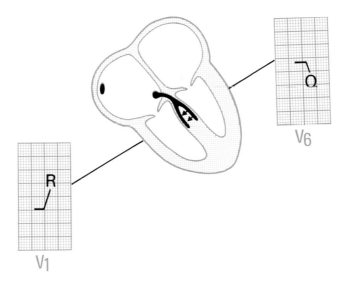

In a right ventricular lead there is then a downward deflection (S wave) as the main muscle mass is depolarised, the bigger left ventricle (in which depolarisation is spreading away from a right ventricular lead) outweighing the effects of the smaller right ventricle (in which depolarisation is moving towards a right ventricular lead). In a left ventricular lead there is an upward deflection (R wave) as the ventricular muscle is depolarised.

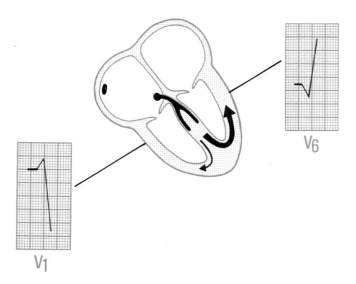

When the whole of the myocardium is depolarised the ECG returns to baseline.

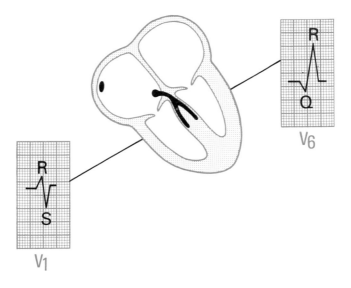

The QRS complex in the chest leads therefore shows a steady progression from $V_1$, where it is predominantly downwards, to $V_6$ where it is predominantly upwards. The 'transition point', where the S and R waves are equal, indicates the position of the interventricular septum.

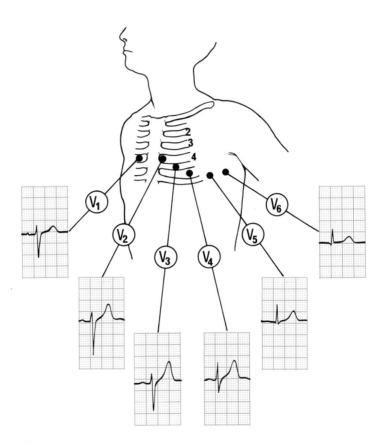

**Things to remember**

1   The ECG results from electrical changes associated with activation first of the atria and then of the ventricles.
2   Atrial activation causes the P wave.
3   Ventricular activation causes the QRS complex. If the first deflection is down it is a Q. If the first deflection is up it is an R. A downwards deflection after an R is an S.

4   When the depolarisation wave spreads towards a lead the deflection is upwards.
5   The six limb leads (I, II, III, VR, VL and VF) look at the heart from the sides and the feet in a vertical plane. The cardiac axis is the average direction of spread of depolarisation as seen from the front, and is estimated from leads, I, II and III.
6   The chest or V leads look at the heart from the front and the left side in a horizontal plane. $V_1$ is positioned over the right ventricle, $V_6$ over the left ventricle.
7   The septum is depolarised from the left side to the right.
8   The left ventricle exerts more influence on the ECG than the right ventricle.

## Chapter 2
# Conduction and its problems

We have already seen that electrical activation normally begins in the sinoatrial node, and that a wave of depolarisation spreads outwards through the atrial muscle to the atrioventricular node, and thence down the His bundle and its branches to the ventricles. The conduction of this wave front can be delayed or blocked at any point. However –

### Principles
1  The ECG is easy to understand.
2  Conduction problems are simple to analyse provided you keep the wiring diagram of the heart constantly in mind.

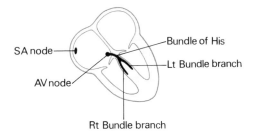

SA node

AV node

Bundle of His

Lt Bundle branch

Rt Bundle branch

We can think of conduction problems in the order in which the depolarisation wave normally spreads — AV node, His bundle, and bundle branches. Remember in all that follows that we are assuming depolarisation begins as usual, in the sinoatrial node.

### 1  Conduction problems in the AV node and His bundle

The time taken by the spread of depolarisation from the SA node to the ventricular muscle is shown by the PR interval (Ch. 1) and is not normally greater than 0.2 s (one large square). Interference with the conduction process causes the ECG phenomenon called 'heart block'.

If each wave of depolarisation that originates in the SA node is conducted to the ventricles but there is delay somewhere along the conduction pathway, then the PR interval is prolonged and this is called *first degree heart block.*

## FIRST DEGREE BLOCK
### PR 0.36 s

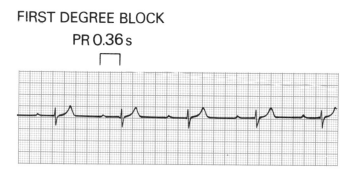

*Note:*  One P wave per QRS complex
PR interval 0.36 s

First degree heart block is not of itself important, but it may be a sign of coronary artery disease, acute rheumatic carditis, digitalis toxicity or electrolyte disturbances.

Sometimes excitation completely fails to pass through the AV node or the bundle of His. When this occurs intermittently *second degree heart block* is said to exist. There are three variations of this:

(a) Most beats are conducted with a constant PR interval, but occasionally there is an atrial contraction without a subsequent ventricular contraction. This is called the 'Mobitz type 2' phenomenon.

## SECOND DEGREE BLOCK

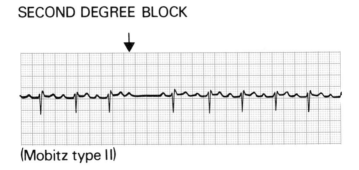

(Mobitz type II)

*Note:* PR interval of the conducted beats is constant. One P wave is not followed by a QRS complex and here 'second degree' block is occurring.

(b) There may be progressive lengthening of the PR
    interval and then failure of conduction of an atrial
    beat, followed by a conducted beat with a short
    PR interval and then a repetition of this cycle. This
    is the 'Wenkebach phenomenon'.

## SECOND DEGREE BLOCK

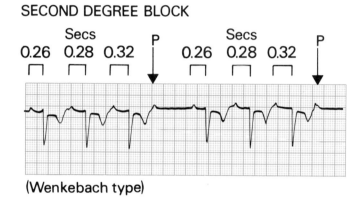

(Wenkebach type)

*Note:*   Progressive lengthening of PR interval
         One non-conducted beat
         Next conducted beat has a shorter PR
         interval

(c) There may be alternate conducted and
    non-conducted atrial beats (or one conducted
    atrial beat and then two non-conducted beats),

giving twice (or three times) as many P waves as QRS complexes. This is called '2 to 1' (or '3 to 1') conduction.

## SECOND DEGREE BLOCK (2:1type)

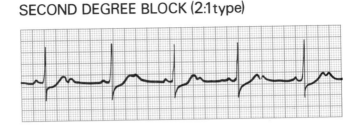

*Note:*   Two P waves per QRS complex
        Normal, and constant, PR interval in the
        conducted beats

It is important to remember with this, as with any other rhythm, that a P wave may only show itself as a distortion of a T wave.

## SECOND DEGREE BLOCK (2:1type)

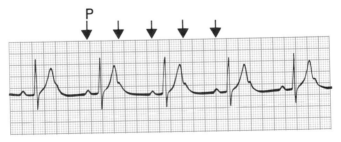

*Note:*   P wave in the T wave can be identified
        because of its regularity

The causes of second degree heart block are the same as those of first degree block. In patients with heart attacks the Wenkebach phenomenon is usually benign, but Mobitz type 2 block and 2 to 1 block may herald complete, or third degree, heart block.

*Complete heart block* (third degree block) is said to occur when atrial contraction is normal but no beats are conducted to the ventricles. When this occurs the ventricles are excited by a slow 'escape mechanism' (see Ch. 3), with a depolarising focus within the ventricular muscle.

## THIRD DEGREE (COMPLETE) BLOCK

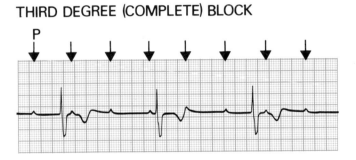

*Note:*   P wave rate 90 per minute
QRS rate 36 per minute
No relation between P and QRS
Abnormal shaped QRS complexes because of abnormal spread of depolarisation from a ventricular focus

Complete heart block may occur as an acute phenomenon in patients with myocardial infarction (when it is usually transient) or it may be a chronic state, usually due to fibrosis around the bundle of His.

## 2    Conduction problems in the right and left bundle branches — bundle branch block

If the depolarisation wave reaches the interventricular septum normally, then the interval between the beginning of the P wave and the first deflection in the QRS complex (the PR interval) will be normal. However, if there is abnormal conduction through either the right or left bundle branches there will be a delay in the depolarisation of part of the ventricular muscle. The extra time taken for depolarisation of the whole of the ventricular muscle causes widening of the QRS complex.

In the normal heart the time taken for the depolarisation wave to spread from the interventricular septum to the furthest part of the ventricles is not more than 0.12 s, or 3 small squares on ECG paper. If the QRS duration is greater than 0.12 s, then conduction within the ventricles must have occurred by an abnormal and therefore slow pathway. When depolarisation has begun in the SA node a wide QRS complex indicates bundle branch block, but we shall see in Chapter 3 that widening also occurs if depolarisation begins within the ventricular muscle itself. Remember that in sinus rhythm with bundle branch block normal P waves are present with a constant PR interval; we shall see that this is not the case with rhythms beginning in the ventricles.

Block of both bundle branches has the same effect as block of the His bundle and causes complete (third degree) heart block.

Right bundle branch block (RBBB) often indicates problems in the right side of the heart, but RBBB patterns with a normal duration of the QRS complex are quite common in healthy people. Left bundle branch block (LBBB) is always an indication of heart disease, usually of the left side. It is important to recognise that bundle branch block is present, for LBBB prevents any further interpretation of the cardiogram, and RBBB can make interpretation difficult.

The mechanism underlying the ECG patterns of right and left bundle branch block can be worked out from first principles. Remember (Ch. 1):

(a)  The septum is normally depolarised from left to right.

(b)  The left ventricle, having the greater muscle mass, exerts more influence on the ECG than the right ventricle.

(c)  Excitation spreading towards a lead causes an upward deflection of the ECG.

## *Right bundle branch block*

No conduction occurs down the right bundle branch, but the septum is depolarised from the left side as usual, causing an R wave in a right ventricular lead ($V_1$) and a small Q in a left ventricular lead ($V_6$).

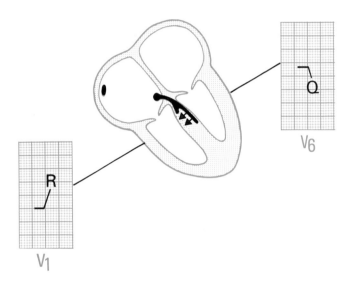

Excitation then spreads to the left ventricle, causing an S in $V_1$ and an R in $V_6$.

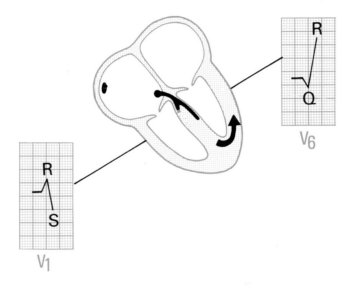

It takes longer for excitation to reach the right ventricle because of the failure of the normal conducting pathway, and the right ventricle therefore depolarises after the left. Therefore there is a second R wave ($R^1$) in $V_1$, and a wide and deep S in $V_6$.

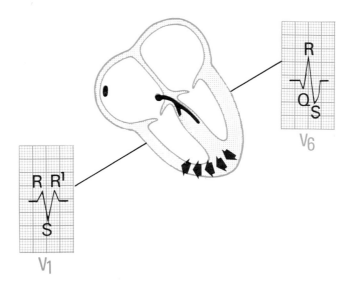

## *Left bundle branch block*

If conduction down the left bundle branch fails, the septum has to be depolarised from right to left, causing a small Q in V$_1$, and an R in V$_6$.

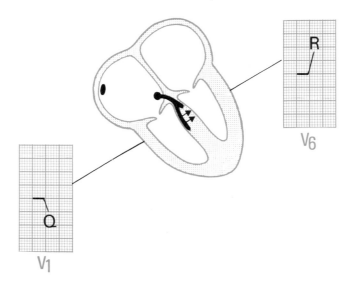

The right ventricle is depolarised before the left, so despite the smaller muscle mass there is an R in V₁ and an S (often appearing only as a notch) in V₆.

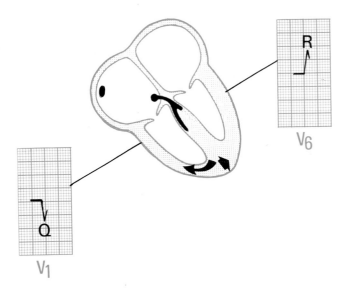

Later depolarisation of the left ventricle causes an S in $V_1$ and another R in $V_6$.

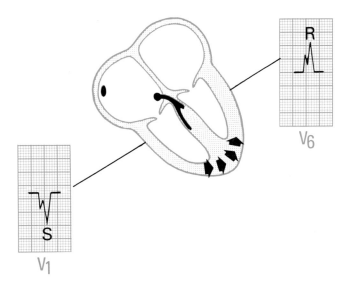

*What to remember*

RBBB is best seen in V$_1$ where there is an RSR pattern.

## RIGHT BUNDLE BRANCH BLOCK

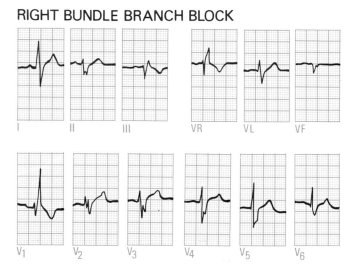

LBBB is best seen in V₆, where there is an M pattern.

## LEFT BUNDLE BRANCH BLOCK

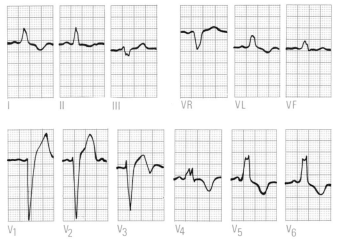

## 3   Conduction problems in the distal parts of the left bundle branch

At this point it is worth considering in a little more detail the anatomy of the branches of the His bundle. The right bundle branch has no main divisions but the left bundle branch has two — the anterior and posterior fascicles. The depolarisation wave therefore spreads into the ventricles by three routes:

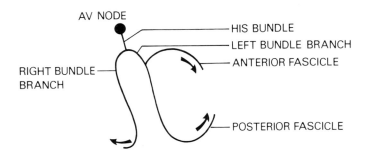

The cardiac axis (Ch. 1) depends on the average direction of depolarisation of the ventricles. Since the left ventricle contains more muscle than the right, it has more influence on the cardiac axis.

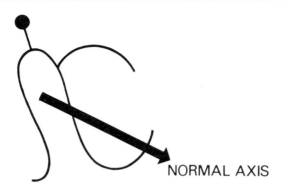

NORMAL AXIS

If the anterior fascicle of the left bundle branch fails to conduct, the left ventricle has to be depolarised through the posterior fascicle and so the cardiac axis rotates upwards.

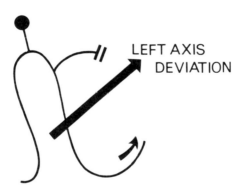

LEFT AXIS
DEVIATION

'Left axis deviation' is therefore due to left anterior fascicular block, or 'left anterior hemiblock'.

The posterior fascicle of the left bundle is not often selectively blocked, but if this does occur the ECG shows right axis deviation.

When the right bundle branch is blocked the cardiac axis is usually normal, because there is normal depolarisation of the left ventricle with its large muscle mass.

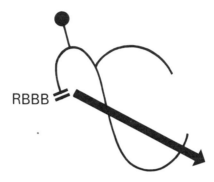

However, if both the right bundle branch and the left anterior fascicle are blocked, the ECG shows right bundle branch block and left axis deviation.

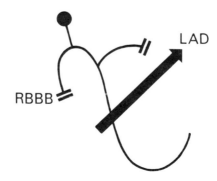

This is sometimes called 'bi-fascicular block', and this particular ECG pattern obviously indicates widespread damage to the conducting system.

If the right bundle branch and both fascicles of the left bundle branch are blocked, complete heart block occurs just as if the main His bundle had failed to conduct.

**Things to remember**

1  Depolarisation normally begins in the SA node, and spreads to the ventricles via the AV node, the His bundle, the right and left branches of the His bundle, and the anterior and posterior fascicles of the left bundle branch.

2  A conduction abnormality can develop at any of these points.

3  Conduction problems in the AV node and His bundle may be partial (first and second degree block) or complete (third degree block).

4  If conduction is normal through the AV node, the His bundle and one of its branches, but is abnormal in the other branch, bundle branch block exists and the QRS complex is wide.

5  The ECG pattern of RBBB and LBBB can be worked out if you remember (a) that the septum is depolarised first from left to right, (b) that $V_1$ looks at the right ventricle and $V_6$ at the left ventricle and (c) that when depolarisation spreads towards an electrode the stylus moves upwards.

6  If you can't remember all this, remember that RBBB has an RSR pattern in $V_1$, while LBBB has an 'M' pattern in $V_6$.

7  Block of the anterior division or fascicle of the left bundle branch causes left axis deviation.

## Chapter 3
# The rhythm of the heart

So far we have only considered the spread of depolarisation that follows the normal activation of the SA node. When depolarisation begins in the SA node the heart is said to be in 'sinus rhythm'. Depolarisation can, however, begin in other places, and then the rhythm is named after the part of the heart where the depolarisation sequence originates.

**Principles**

1   The ECG is easy to understand.
2   Abnormalities of cardiac rhythm are particularly easy to work out, and the key is the P wave.

When attempting to analyse a cardiac rhythm remember:

(a) atrial contraction is associated with the P wave, of the ECG,
(b) ventricular contraction is associated with the QRS complex,
(c) atrial contraction normally precedes ventricular contraction, and there is normally one atrial contraction per ventricular contraction (i.e. there

should be as many P waves as there are QRS
complexes.)

## The intrinsic rhythmicity of the heart

Most parts of the heart can depolarise spontaneously
and rhythmically, and the rate of contraction of the
ventricles will be controlled by the part of the heart
that is depolarising most frequently. The sino-atrial
(SA) node normally has the highest frequency of
discharge and therefore the rate of contraction of the
ventricles will follow that of the SA node.

The rate of discharge of the SA node is influenced
by the vagus nerves and reflexes originating in the
lung affect the heart rate. Changes in rate associated
with respiration are normally seen in young people,
and this is called *sinus arrhythmia.*

## SINUS ARRHYTHMIA

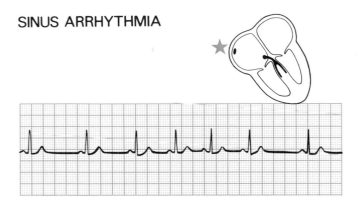

*Note:*   One P wave per QRS complex
          Constant PR interval
          Progressive beat-to-beat change in R–R
          interval

A slow sinus rhythm (sinus bradycardia) is associated with athletic training, fainting attacks, hypothermia, myxoedema, and it is often seen immediately after a heart attack. A fast sinus rhythm (sinus tachycardia) is associated with exercise, fear, pain, haemorrhage and thyrotoxicosis. There is no particular rate that is called 'bradycardia' or 'tachycardia'; these are merely descriptive terms.

Abnormal cardiac rhythms can begin in three places — the atrial muscle, the region around the AV node (these rhythms are called 'nodal' or more properly, 'junctional') and in the ventricular muscle.

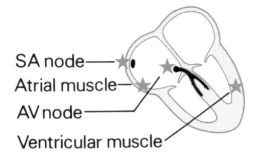

Sinus rhythm, atrial rhythms, and junctional rhythms together constitute the 'supraventricular' rhythms.

In the supraventricular rhythms the depolarisation wave spreads to the ventricles in the normal way via the His bundle and its branches. The QRS complex is therefore normal, and is the same whether depolarisation was initiated by the SA node, the atrial muscle, or the junctional region.

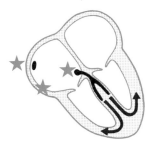

In ventricular rhythms, on the other hand, the depolarisation wave spreads through the ventricles by an abnormal and therefore slow pathway. The QRS complex is therefore wide and abnormal. Repolarisation is also abnormal, so the T wave is an abnormal shape.

*Remember*

1.   Supraventricular rhythms have narrow QRS complexes.
2.   Ventricular rhythms have wide complexes.
3.   The only exception to this rule is when there is a supraventricular rhythm with right or left bundle branch block.

## Types of abnormal rhythm

Abnormal rhythms arising in the atrial muscle, the junctional region or the ventricular muscle can be slow and sustained (the bradycardias) or they can occur as early single beats (extrasystoles) or they can be sustained and fast (tachycardias). When activation of the atria or ventricles is totally disorganised, fibrillation is said to exist. We can consider each of these types of rhythm in turn.

*The escape rhythms — the bradycardias*

It is clearly an advantage for different parts of the heart to be able to initiate the depolarisation sequence, for this gives the heart a series of 'fail-safe' mechanisms that will keep it going if the SA node fails to depolarise, or if conduction of the depolarisation wave is blocked. However, the protective mechanisms must normally be switched off if competition between normal and abnormal sites of spontaneous depolarisation is to be avoided. This is achieved by the secondary sites having a lower intrinsic frequency of depolarisation than the SA node. The heart is controlled by whichever site is depolarising itself most frequently: normally this is the SA node and it gives a normal rate of about 70 per minute. If the SA node fails to depolarise control will be assumed by a focus either in the atrial muscle or in the region around the AV node (the 'junctional' region) both of which have spontaneous depolarisation frequencies of about 50 per minute. If these fail, or if conduction through the His bundle is blocked, a ventricular focus will take over and give a ventricular rate of about 30 per minute.

These slow and protective rhythms are called 'escape' rhythms, because they are seen when secondary sites for initiating depolarisation escape from the normal inhibition of the more active SA node.

Escape rhythms are not primary disorders, but are the response to problems higher in the conducting pathway. They are commonly seen in the acute phase of a heart attack, when they may be associated with sinus bradycardia. It is important not to try to suppress an escape rhythm, because without it the heart might stop altogether.

If the SA node slows down and a focus in the atrium takes over control of the heart, the rhythm is described as *atrial escape.* Atrial escape beats can occur singly.

## ATRIAL ESCAPE

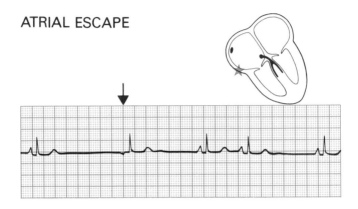

*Note:*   After one sinus beat the SA node fails to depolarise. After a delay an abnormal P wave is seen because excitation of the atrium has begun somewhere away from the SA node. The abnormal P wave is followed by a normal QRS, because excitation has spread normally down the His Bundle. The remaining beats show a return to sinus rhythm

If the region around the AV node takes over, the rhythm is called *nodal*, or more properly, *junctional escape*.

## NODAL (JUNCTIONAL) ESCAPE

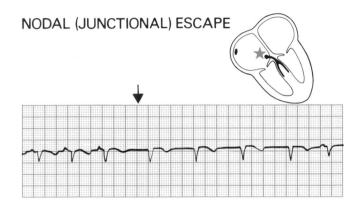

*Note:*   Sinus rate 100 per minute; junctional escape (following arrow) at 70 per minute
No P waves in junctional beats (either no atrial contraction, or P wave lost in QRS)
Normal QRS

*Ventricular escape* most commonly occurs when conduction between the atria and ventricles is interrupted, and complete heart block is the classical ventricular escape rhythm.

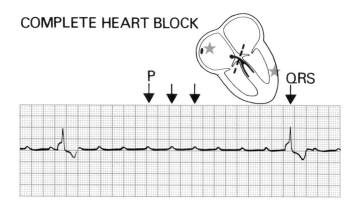

COMPLETE HEART BLOCK

*Note:* Regular P waves (normal atrial depolarisation). P wave rate 145 per minute.
Regular QRS, but complexes highly abnormal because of abnormal conduction through ventricular muscle. QRS (ventricular escape) rate 15 per minute
No relation between P waves and QRS complexes

Ventricular escape beats can be single.

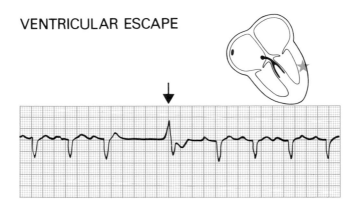

**VENTRICULAR ESCAPE**

*Note:* After three sinus beats the SA node fails to discharge. After a pause there is a single wide and abnormal QRS complex (arrow) with an abnormal T wave. No atrial or junctional escape beat has appeared, and a ventricular focus controls the heart for one beat. Sinus rhythm is then restored.

The rhythm of the heart can occasionally be controlled by a ventricular focus with an intrinsic frequency of discharge faster than that seen in complete heart block. The rhythm is then called 'accelerated idioventricular rhythm'.

## ACCELERATED IDIOVENTRICULAR RHYTHM

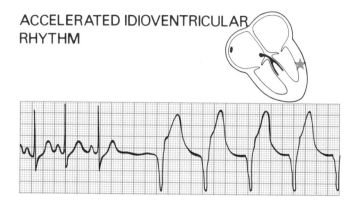

*Note:*   After three sinus beats the SA node fails to depolarise. An escape focus in the ventricles takes over, causing a regular rhythm at 75 per minute with wide QRS complexes and abnormal T waves.

Although the appearance of the ECG is similar to that of ventricular tachycardia (see below) accelerated idioventricular rhythm is benign and should not be treated. Ventricular tachycardia should not be diagnosed unless the heart rate exceeds 120 per minute.

## Extrasystoles

Any part of the heart can depolarise earlier than it should, and the accompanying heart beat is called an extrasystole. The term 'ectopic' is sometimes used to indicate that depolarisation originated in an abnormal place, and the term 'premature contraction' is also used to mean the same thing.

The ECG appearance of an extrasystole arising in the atrial muscle, the junctional or nodal region, or in the ventricular muscle, is the same as that of the corresponding 'escape' beat — the difference is that an extrasystole comes early, and an escape beat comes late.

Atrial extrasystoles have abnormal P waves; a junctional extrasystole either has no P wave at all, or it may appear immediately before or immediately after the QRS complex. The QRS complexes of atrial and junctional extrasystoles are, of course, the same as those of sinus rhythm.

## ATRIAL AND JUNCTIONAL (NODAL) EXTRASYSTOLES

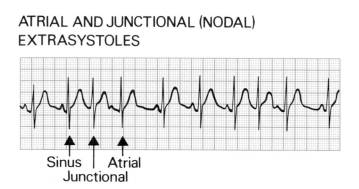

Sinus | Atrial
Junctional

*Note:*   This record shows sinus rhythm with junctional and atrial extrasystoles
Sinus, junctional and atrial beats have identical QRS complexes — conduction in and beyond the bundle of His is normal
A junctional extrasystole has no P wave
An atrial extrasystole has an abnormal-shaped P wave

Ventricular extrasystoles, however, have abnormal QRS complexes. Ventricular extrasystoles are common, and are usually of no importance. However, when they occur early in the T wave of a preceding beat they can induce ventricular fibrillation and are thus potentially dangerous.

## VENTRICULAR EXTRASYSTOLE

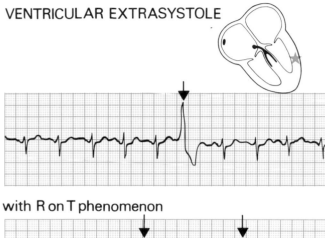

### with R on T phenomenon

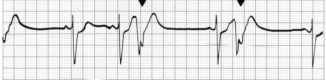

*Note:*   Upper trace shows five sinus beats then an early beat with a wide QRS and an abnormal T wave: this is a ventricular extrasystole. In the lower trace the ventricular extrasystoles occur at the peak of the T waves of the preceding sinus beats: this is the 'R on T' phenomenon

It may, however, not be as easy as this, particularly if a beat of supraventricular origin is conducted abnormally to the ventricles (see bundle branch block — Ch. 2). It is best to get in the habit of asking five questions every time:

1   Does the early QRS complex follow an early P wave? If it does, it must be an atrial extrasystole.

2   Can a P wave be seen anywhere? A junctional extrasystole may cause the appearance of a P wave very close to, and even after, the QRS complex because excitation is conducted both to the atria and to the ventricles.

3   Is the QRS complex the same shape (i.e. has it the same initial direction of deflection as the normal beat, and is it the same duration)? Supraventricular beats look the same, ventricular beats look different.

4   Is the T wave the same way up as in the normal beat? Supraventricular — same. Ventricular — different.

5   Does the next P wave after the extrasystole appear at the expected time? In both supraventricular and ventricular extrasystoles there is a ('compensatory') pause before the next heart beat, but a supraventricular extrasystole usually upsets the normal periodicity of the SA node, so that the next SA node discharge (and P wave) comes late.

The effects of supraventricular and ventricular extrasystoles on the following P wave are seen in the next two examples.

A supraventricular extrasystole resets the P wave cycle:

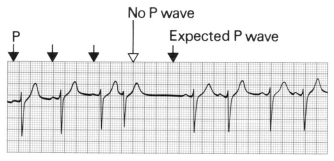

SUPRAVENTRICULAR EXTRASYSTOLE

No P wave

P          Expected P wave

*Note:*   Three sinus beats are followed by a junctional extrasystole. No P wave is seen at the expected time. After the compensatory pause the next P wave is late.

A ventricular extrasystole, on the other hand, does not affect the SA node so the next P wave appears at the predicted time.

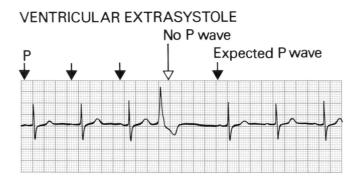

### VENTRICULAR EXTRASYSTOLE

*Note:* Three sinus beats are followed by a ventricular extrasystole. No P wave is seen after this beat but the next P wave arrives on time.

**The tachycardias — the fast rhythms**

Foci in the atria, the junctional (AV nodal) region, and ventricles may fire repeatedly, causing a sustained tachycardia. The criteria already described can be used to decide the origin of the arrhythmia, and as before the most important thing is to try to identify a P wave.

*(a) Supraventricular tachycardias*

*1   Atrial tachycardia (abnormal focus in the atrium)*

In atrial tachycardia the atria contract faster than 150 per minute.

ATRIAL TACHYCARDIA

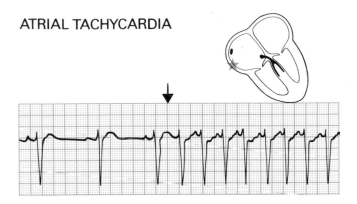

*Note:*   After three sinus beats atrial tachycardia develops at a rate of 160 per minute. P waves can be seen superimposed on the T waves of the preceding beats. The QRS complexes and T waves have the same shape as the sinus beats.

The AV node cannot conduct atrial rates above about 200 per minute, so if the atrial rate is faster than this atrio-ventricular block occurs. When the atrial rate is above 250, and there is no flat baseline between P waves, *atrial flutter* is present.

## ATRIAL FLUTTER (4:1)

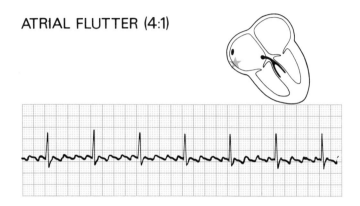

*Note:*   P waves can be seen at 300 per minute, giving a 'saw-tooth' appearance. There are four P waves per QRS complex, and ventricular activation is perfectly regular at 75 per minute.

When atrial tachycardia or atrial flutter is associated with 2:1 block it is easy to fail to recognise the extra P waves.

## ATRIAL FLUTTER (2:1)

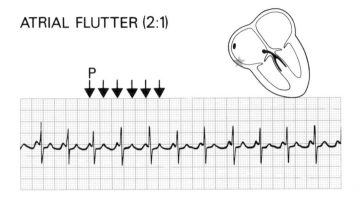

*Note:*   Atrial flutter with an atrial rate of 300 per minute is present and there is 2:1 block giving a ventricular rate of 150 per minute. The first of the two P waves associated with each QRS can be confused with the T waves of the preceding beat, but P waves can be identified from their regularity.

*Carotid sinus pressure* may have a useful therapeutic effect on supraventricular tachycardias, and is always worth trying as it may make the nature of the arrhythmia more obvious.

## ATRIAL FLUTTER WITH CAROTID SINUS PRESSURE (CSP)

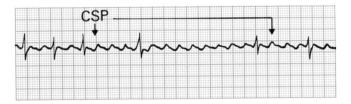

*Note:*   In this case, carotid sinus pressure has increased the block between atria and ventricles, and has made it obvious that the underlying rhythm is atrial flutter

## 2  Junctional ('nodal') tachycardia

If the area around the AV node depolarises frequently, the P waves may be seen very close to the QRS (as with the corresponding extrasystoles) or may not be seen at all. The QRS complex is of normal shape because, as with the other supraventricular arrhythmias, the ventricles are activated down the Bundle of His in the normal way.

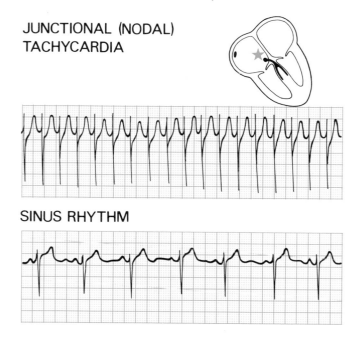

JUNCTIONAL (NODAL) TACHYCARDIA

SINUS RHYTHM

*Note:*  In the upper trace there is no P wave and the QRS complexes are completely regular at 200 per minute. The lower trace is from the same patient, in sinus rhythm. The QRS complexes have the same shape as those of the junctional tachycardia.

## (b) Ventricular tachycardias

If a focus in the ventricular muscle depolarises at high frequency (causing, in effect, rapidly repeated ventricular extrasystoles) the rhythm is called ventricular tachycardia. Excitation has to spread by an abnormal path through the ventricular muscle, and the QRS complex is wide and abnormal.

VENTRICULAR TACHYCARDIA

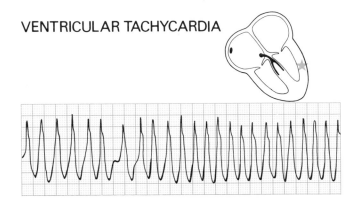

*Note:*   No P waves
Wide QRS complexes
QRS complexes slightly irregular and vary slightly in shape

Remember that wide and abnormal complexes are also seen with bundle branch block.

### SINUS RHYTHM WITH LEFT BUNDLE BRANCH BLOCK

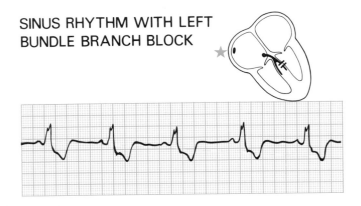

*Note:*   Sinus rhythm: each QRS is preceded by a P wave with a constant PR interval. The QRS complexes are wide and the T waves are inverted. In a single lead it is not possible to differentiate left and right bundle branch block

## Fibrillation

All the arrhythmias so far discussed have involved the synchronous contraction of all the muscle fibres of the atria or of the ventricles, albeit at abnormal speeds. When individual muscle fibres contract independently they are said to be 'fibrillating'. Fibrillation can occur in the atrial or ventricular muscle.

When the atrial muscle fibres contract independently there are no P waves on the ECG but only an irregular line. At times there may be 'flutter'-like waves for 2 or 3 seconds. The AV node is continuously bombarded with depolarisation waves of varying strength, and depolarisation spreads at irregular intervals down the bundle of His. The AV node conducts in an 'all or none' fashion so that the depolarisation waves passing into the His bundle are of constant intensity. However, these waves are irregular and the ventricles therefore contract irregularly. Because conduction into and through the ventricles is by the normal route, each QRS complex is a normal shape.

# ATRIAL FIBRILLATION

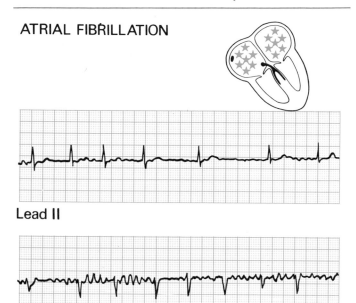

Lead II

Lead V₁

*Note:*   No P waves  — irregular baseline
Irregular QRS complexes
Normal shaped QRS
In lead V₁ 'flutter'-like waves can be seen
transiently: this is common in atrial fibrillation.

## *Ventricular fibrillation*

When the ventricular muscle fibres contract independently no QRS complex can be identified and the ECG is totally disorganised.

## VENTRICULAR FIBRILLATION

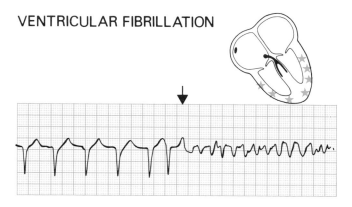

As the patient will usually have lost consciousness by the time you have realised that it is not just due to a loose connection, the diagnosis is easy.

## The Wolff–Parkinson–White (WPW) syndrome

The only normal electrical connection between the atria and ventricles is the His bundle. Some people, however, have an extra or 'accessory' conducting bundle. These accessory bundles form a direct connection between atrium and ventricle, usually on left side of the heart, and in this acessory bundle there is no AV node to delay conduction. A depolarisation wave therefore reaches the ventricle early, and 'pre-excitation' occurs. The PR interval is short, and the QRS shows an early slurred upstroke called a delta wave. The second part of the QRS is normal as conduction through the His bundle catches up with the pre-excitation.

The only clinical importance of this anatomical abnormality is that it can cause paroxysmal tachycardia. Depolarisation can spread down the accessory bundle and back up the His bundle and so reactivates the atrium. A 're-entry' circuit is thus set up, and a sustained tachycardia occurs.

# WOLFF-PARKINSON-WHITE SYNDROME

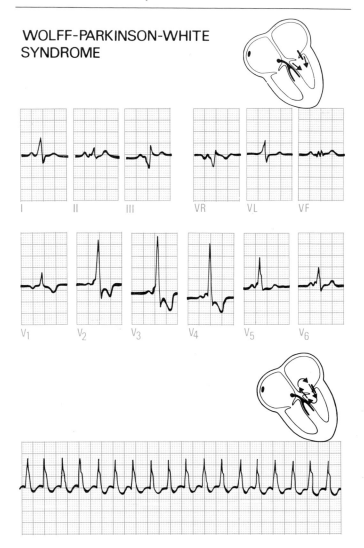

*Note:*   The 12 lead ECG shows sinus rhythm
The PR interval is short
There is a slurred upstroke of the QRS
The dominant R in $V_1$ and the inverted T in the anterior chest leads are characteristic of the WPW syndrome
During re-entry tachycardia no P waves can be seen

We have considered the tachycardias up to now as if all were due to an increased spontaneous frequency of depolarisation of some part of the heart. While such an 'enhanced automaticity' certainly accounts for some tachycardias, others are due to re-entry circuits within the heart muscle. However, it is not possible to distinguish enhanced automaticity from re-entry on standard ECGs, and fortunately this differentiation has no practical importance.

**Things to remember about rhythms**

1   Most parts of the heart are capable of spontaneous depolarisation.
2   Abnormal rhythms can arise in the atrial muscle, the region around the AV node (the 'junctional' region) and in the ventricular muscle.
3   Escape rhythms are slow, and are protective.
4   Occasional early depolarisation of any part of the heart causes an extrasystole.
5   Frequent depolarisation of any part of the heart causes a tachycardia.
6   Asynchronous contraction of muscle fibres in the atria or ventricles is called fibrillation.

7   Apart from the rate, the ECG pattern of an escape rhythm, an extrasystole, and a tachycardia arising in any one part of the heart is the same.

8   All supraventricular rhythms have normal QRS complexes provided there is no bundle branch block (Ch. 2).

9   Ventricular rhythms cause wide and abnormal QRS complexes, and abnormal T waves.

Recognising ECG abnormalities is to a large extent like recognising an elephant — once seen, never forgotten. However, in cases of difficulty it is helpful to ask the following questions, referring to Table 1.

(a)  Is the abnormality occasional or sustained?
(b)  Are there any P Waves?
(c)  Are there as many QRS complexes as P waves?
(d)  Are the ventricles contracting regularly or irregularly?
(e)  Is the QRS complex a normal shape?
(f)   What is the ventricular rate?

Table 1 gives a flow diagram for analysing rhythm and conduction abnormalities. It also shows the most basic methods for treating arrhythmias, using only lignocaine, atropine and digoxin. It is worth remembering that many abnormalities of cardiac rhythm can be induced by too much digoxin, and if a patient on digoxin develops an arrhythmia the first thing to do is to stop this drug.

**Table 1**

| Abnormality | P wave | P:QRS ratio | QRS regularity | QRS shape | QRS rate | Rhythm | First line treatment |
|---|---|---|---|---|---|---|---|
| Occasional | (i.e. extrasystoles) | | | Normal | | Supraventricular | Nothing |
| | | | | Abnormal | | Ventricular | Nothing or lignocaine |
| Sustained | Present | P's = QRS's | Regular | Normal | Normal | Sinus rhythm | Nothing |
| | | | | | 160 + | Atrial tachycardia | Digoxin |
| | | | Slightly irregular | Normal | Normal | Sinus arrhythmia | Nothing |
| | | More P's than QRS's | Regular | Normal | Slow | Atrial escape | Atropine |
| | | | | | Fast | Atrial tachycardia with block | Digoxin |
| | | | | | Slow | 2° Heart block | Nothing |
| | | | | Abnormal | Slow | Complete heart block | Hospital |
| | Absent | | Regular | Normal | Fast | Nodal tachycardia | Digoxin |
| | | | | | Slow | Nodal escape | Atropine |
| | | | | Abnormal | Fast | Nodal tachycardia with bundle branch block | Hospital |
| | | | Slightly irregular | Abnormal | Fast | Ventricular tachycardia | Lignocaine then hospital |
| | QRS absent | | Very irregular | Normal | Any speed | Atrial fibrillation Ventricular fibrillation or standstill | Digoxin Cardiac massage |

## Chapter 4

# Abnormalities of the P, QRS and T waves

When interpreting an ECG, identify the rhythm first. Then ask the following questions — always in the same sequence:

1   Are there any abnormalities of the P wave?
2   What is the cardiac axis? (Look at the QRS in leads, I, II, III — and at chapter 1 if necessary.)
3   Is the QRS of normal duration?
4   Are there any other abnormalities in the QRS – particularly, are there any Q waves?
5   Is the ST segment raised or depressed?
6   Is the T wave normal?

**Principles**

1   The ECG is easy to understand.
2   The P wave can only be normal, unusually tall, or unusually broad.
3   The QRS complex can only have three abnormalities — it can be too broad, too tall, and it may contain an abnormal Q wave.
4   The ST segment can only be normal, elevated or depressed.
5   The T wave can only be the right way up or the wrong way up.

## Abnormalities of the P Wave

Apart from alterations of the shape of the P wave associated with rhythm changes, there are only two important abnormalities:

1   Anything that causes the right atrium to become hypertrophied (tricuspid valve stenosis, or pulmonary hypertension) causes the P to become peaked.

## RIGHT ATRIAL HYPERTROPHY

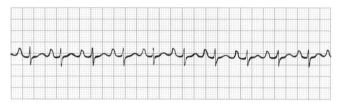

2   Left atrial hypertrophy (usually due to mitral stenosis) causes a broad and bifid P wave.

## LEFT ATRIAL HYPERTROPHY

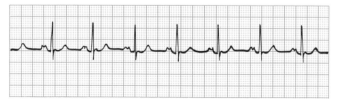

**Abnormalities of the QRS complex**

The normal QRS complex has four characteristics:

(a) its duration is no greater than 0.12 s (3 small squares)

(b) in a right ventricular lead ($V_1$) the S wave is greater than the R wave

(c) in a left ventricular lead ($V_5$ or $V_6$) the height of the R wave is less than 25 mm

(d) left ventricular leads may show Q waves due to septal depolarisation, but these are less than 1 mm across and less than 2 mm deep

*1   Abnormalities of the width of the QRS complex*

QRS complexes are abnormally wide in the presence of bundle branch block (Ch. 2), or when depolarisation is initiated by a focus in the ventricular muscle (Ch. 3). In either case the increased width indicates that depolarisation has spread through the ventricles by an abnormal and therefore slow pathway.

*2   Increased height of the QRS complex*

An increase of muscle mass in either ventricle will lead to increased electrical activity, and to an increase in the height of the QRS complex.

*Right ventricular hypertrophy* is best seen in the right ventricular leads (especially $V_1$). Since the left ventricle does not have its usual dominant effect on the QRS shape, the complex becomes upright (i.e. the height of the R wave exceeds the depth of the S) — this is always abnormal. There will be a deep S in $V_6$.

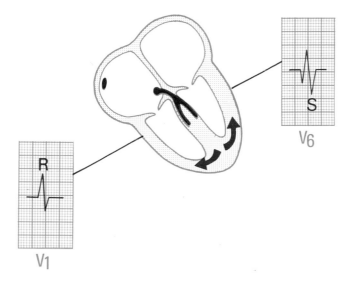

This is usually accompanied by right axis deviation (Ch. 1), by a peaked P wave (right atrial hypertrophy), and in severe cases by inversion of the T waves in $V_2$ and $V_3$.

## RIGHT VENTRICULAR HYPERTROPHY

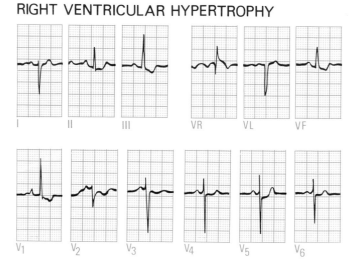

In *pulmonary embolism* the ECG may show features of right ventricular hypertrophy, although in many cases there is nothing abnormal other than a sinus tachycardia. When pulmonary embolus is suspected, look for

(a) peaked P waves
(b) right axis deviation
(c) tall R waves in $V_1$

(d) right bundle branch block
(e) inverted T waves in $V_1$ (normal) spreading across to $V_2$ or $V_3$
(f) a shift of transition point to the left, so that the R wave equals the S wave in $V_5$ or $V_6$ rather than in $V_3$ or $V_4$
(g) curiously, a Q wave in lead 3 resembling an inferior infarction

*Left ventricular hypertrophy* causes a tall R wave (greater than 25 mm in $V_5$ or $V_6$) and a deep S in $V_1$ or $V_2$ — but in practice such 'voltage' changes alone are unhelpful in diagnosing left ventricular enlargement. With significant hypertrophy there are also inverted T waves in $V_5$ and $V_6$ and there may be left axis deviation.

## LEFT VENTRICULAR HYPERTROPHY

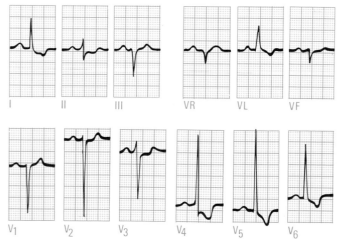

## 3   The origin of Q waves

Small ('septal') Q waves in the left ventricular leads result from depolarisation of the septum from left to right (Ch. 1). However, Q waves greater than 0.04 s (one small square) in width and greater than 2 mm in depth have a quite different significance.

The ventricles are depolarised from inside outwards. Therefore an electrode placed in the cavity of a ventricle would record only a Q wave, as all the depolarisation waves would be moving away from it. If a myocardial infarction causes complete death of muscle from the inside surface to the outside surface of the heart, an electrical 'window' is created, and an electrode looking at the heart over that window will record a cavity potential — that is, a Q wave.

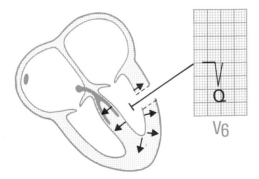

Q waves greater than one small square across and/or more than 2 mm deep therefore indicate a myocardial infarction, and the leads in which the Q wave appears give some indication of the part of the heart that has been damaged. Thus, infarction of the anterior wall of the left ventricle causes a Q wave in the leads looking at the heart from the front — $V_3$ and $V_4$ (Ch. 1).

## ANTERIOR INFARCTION

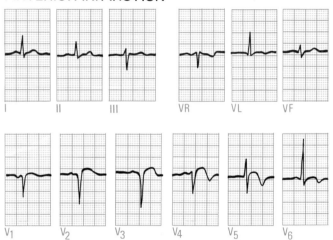

If the infarction involves both the anterior and lateral surfaces of the heart, a Q wave will be present in $V_3$ and $V_4$ and in the leads that 'look at' the lateral surface — I, $V_2$ and $V_{5-6}$.

## ANTERO-LATERAL INFARCTION

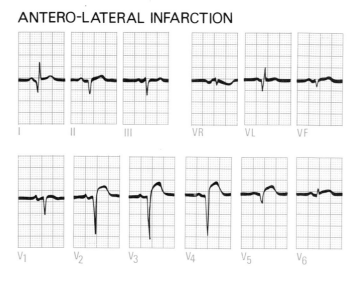

Infarctions of the inferior surface of the heart cause Q waves in the leads looking at the heart from below — III and VF.

## INFERIOR INFARCTION

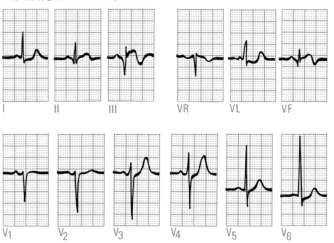

The presence of a Q wave does not, however, give any indication of the age of the infarction, for once a Q wave has developed it is usually permanent.

### Abnormalities of the ST segment

The ST segment lies between the QRS complex and the T wave.

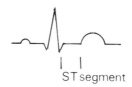

ST segment

It should be 'isoelectric' — that is, at the same level as the part between the T and the next P — but it may be elevated

ST elevated

or depressed.

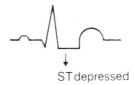

ST depressed

*Elevation* of the ST segment is an indication of acute myocardial injury, usually due either to a recent infarction or to pericarditis. Again, the leads in which it occurs indicate the part of the heart that is damaged — anterior damage shows in the V leads, and inferior in III and VF. Pericarditis is not usually a localised affair, and therefore it causes ST elevation in most leads.

*Horizontal depression* of the ST segment, association with an upright T wave, is usually a sign of ischaemia as opposed to infarction. When the ECG at rest is normal, ST segment depression may appear on effort, particularly when effort induces angina.

## EXERCISE-INDUCED ISCHAEMIC CHANGES

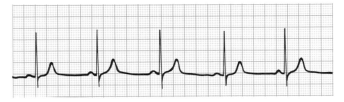

Rest

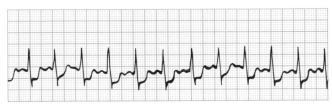

Exercise

## Abnormalities of the T wave

The T wave may be lengthened or made taller by electrolyte (especially potassium) abnormalities. Low plasma potassium levels flatten the T wave and prolong the QT interval (the duration from the Q wave to the end of the T wave) to more than 0.4 seconds.

The most common abnormality is inversion of the T wave, which is seen in the following circumstances:

1   *Normality.* The T wave is normally inverted in VR and in $V_1$ (and in $V_2$ in young people, and also in $V_3$ in some Negroes).

2   *Ischaemia.* After a myocardial infarction the first abnormality seen on the ECG is elevation of the ST segment. Subsequently Q waves appear, and the T wave becomes inverted. The ST segment returns to the baseline, the whole process taking a variable time but usually 24–48 hours. T wave inversion is often permanent.

# DEVELOPMENT OF INFERIOR INFARCTION

## Pain for 1 hour

## Pain for 6 hours

## 24 hours later

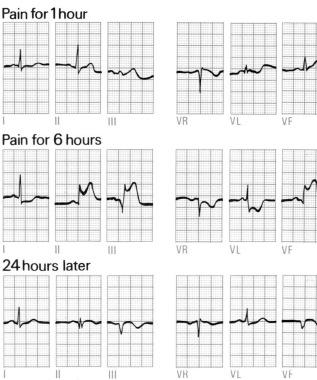

If an infarction is not 'full-thickness' and so does not cause an electrical window, there will be T wave inversion but no Q waves. This is called a 'subendocardial infarction' pattern.

## SUBENDOCARDIAL INFARCTION

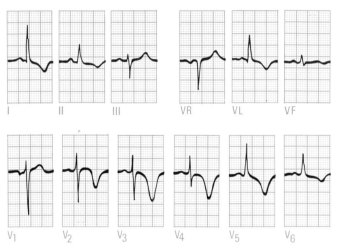

3   *Ventricular hypertrophy.* Left ventricular hypertrophy causes inverted T waves in leads looking at the left ventricle (V$_5$, V$_6$, II and VL). (See above.) Right ventricular hypertrophy causes

T wave inversion in the leads looking at the right ventricle (T inversion is normal in $V_1$ but in white adults is abnormal in $V_2$ or $V_3$).

4   *Bundle branch block.* The abnormal path of depolarisation in bundle branch block is usually associated with an abnormal path of repolarisation.

Therefore, inverted T waves associated with QRS complexes 0.16 s or more in duration have no significance of themselves.

5   *Digoxin.* The administration of digoxin causes T inversion, particularly with sloping depression of the ST segment. It is helpful to record an ECG *before* beginning digitalis to save later confusion about the significance of T wave changes.

## DIGITALIS EFFECT

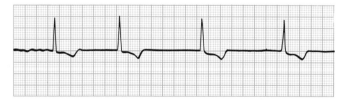

6   *Non-specific changes.* Minor abnormalities of ST segment and T wave (T wave flattening, etc.) are usually of no great significance, and are best reported as 'non-specific ST–T changes'.

## Things to remember

1   Tall P waves result from right atrial hypertrophy, and broad P waves from left atrial hypertrophy.

2   Broadening of the QRS complex indicates abnormal intraventricular conduction: it is seen in bundle branch block and in complexes originating in the ventricular muscle.

3   Increased height of the QRS complex indicates ventricular hypertrophy. Right ventricular hypertrophy is seen in $V_1$ and left ventricular hypertrophy is seen in $V_5$ and $V_6$.

4   Q waves greater than 1 mm across and 2 mm deep indicate myocardial infarction.

5   ST segment elevation indicates acute myocardial infarction or pericarditis.

6   ST segment depression and T wave inversion may be due to ischaemia, ventricular hypertrophy abnormal intraventricular conduction, or digitalis.

## Conclusions

1   The ECG is easy to understand.

2   Most abnormalities of the ECG are amenable to reason.

# Further reading

Although the ECG is easy in principle, variations in its appearances can make it seem complex. *The ECG in Practice* is a companion volume to the *The ECG Made Easy*, and it has been written to help you make the most of the ECG — and to appreciate its limitations.

Hampton J R 1986 The ECG in practice. Churchill Livingstone, Edinburgh

# Index